for Ira,

who understands.

— Roland Labrie

Reaching For Quiet

Poems by
Roland Labrie

Designed and produced by Maine Authors Publishing, Rockland, Maine
www.MaineAuthorsPublishing.com

Printed in the United States of America

for the reader

thou away, the very birds are mute
W.S., XCVII

Contents

III
No Absence Can Be Real

IV
So All At Sea

I

Mark The Years

Taking Down The Tree

This is about why
we can't matter-of-factly
lay these splendid trifles away
without a thought
for the far-between trees
that light the long winter nights
and mark the years in too-fews,

these masters of camouflage
gleaming through their smudges,
nesting in for the long wait
until next time, next time,
glitter dampened in dog-eared boxes
under so-far-gone cellophane,

under cover,
repeating for some maybe next year:
once more, once more,
you've seen what we can do.

Down East In November

Blueberry barrens.
The shin-high pile of blued carpet reds,
rough when you really look
at the thin twigwood in scrubby leaf,
the endless folds of it
unrolling one behind the other
into—is it—far Canada?

Red stretching out to sea along the reach
where you don't expect it,
and over the shoulders of the hills
descending
the long ever-leveling swale
into the great boglands below

you've seen it.
That color.
That not quite red on the lips,
or baked on the bottom of the dish,
cooked, crushed, like no other.

October Sunrise

Waking together we see it
seeping along the world's edge,
kindling catching at the flaming air,
our trumpet eyes in glory
dancing with the maples
in the orange sunrise shout

—forms now your mouth with soundless wonder—

like sparks
blazing on chips
snapped from the stove
the sun's coming up,
the woods are on fire,
the world is burning.

Apple Picking

Leaning beyond all this business
of ladders and buckets and bins,
the standing and swaying in loaded limbs,
back and forth of elbow and wrist,
trick of the unconscious hand—
ears hear and eyes see
a branch bending in a slight shift,
or distant or close, bird song
among the neighborly hilltops.

The hand can teach the mind
to reach through the view.
Row on row the trees stand up,
rise up in sap-run,
bud and blossom beyond thought,
fruit from the ancient bindings
of air and earth.

Still or quick the hand and heart are one
In September's timeless turning.
In the hand, in the mind, in the heart's eye view
be warm and red and ripe in the sun.

Boys In Summer

Clocks did tick more slowly then.
We smile now remembering
what rituals were at work
in our frog-counting laziness.
We found out
stealing through shady woods
to who-knows-whose back garden—
the delight in all that stealth—
for rhubarb sour and grapes worse,
the real point of it all somehow hidden
within that mysterious overgrown arbor,
enchantment in the great curving questions
of the all-around-us vines.

We found some answers later,
hobble-walking
forbidden railroad tracks,
listening to the wind blowing through
the empty Boston & Maine boxcars
of impossibly stretched August afternoons.

Morning Heat, Haying

Out here, open field
in the high hot sizzle
of crickets shrilling
under a blue band,
a white line of sky light
in on me leaning, low light
ripping open blossom so blue
though I want to that badly
I can't tell you how blue

because I know you never see
the chipped and ragged rim
of windrowed blue vetch
drink this wind
that sifts us dry
to blue-binding July.

Old Roses

These old dooryard roses
can best be found around
cellar holes of old farms
long abandoned,
buildings sometimes burned
or simply fallen in and forgotten.
Wading through field flowers
and brambles and brush
I come upon these stragglers
spindling among sill stones,
straying in forever.

They whisper their nevers, the roses,
to the ruthless woods encroaching,
quenching the light they lust for
through the lazy years.

In summer's memory tightly hugged,
in a deep and truly purple bowl
is a pinkest handful carefully not clenched
all the long walk home.

It is already tomorrow in their flaring hearts
this hasty June, these old farmyard roses,
in their new and final beauty shattering,
faint and wrinkled at their edges,
petal by petal across the table.

At Long Hill In May

The longer day makes a place of light
and light shade,
an airy space of airy flowers,
thin paths of pine straw
frayed soft,
or mossy unraked corners,
fine unkempt corners.

How tell the kind and age
of old friends met new,
leaf and bark and blossom?
Volunteers escaping bed and border cage
of sometime tended grounds?
There are no bounds.

This long looking back
through tangled orchard trees
and downstrewn walls
only leaves the eye to linger
in the light of the longer day.

O brief but endless look.
Pause.
As your eyes touch, how sing
an old old hill made all now Spring?

Spring Ephemerals

Ranks of emerald croziers
signal the rubrics of succession.
Always first Emily's *bold little beauty,*
pink, small and punctual—
then, like blurred music, the rush.
Sweet white violets in the wetlands,
small as your littlest fingernail is small,
shy anemones in the wispy litter,
lyrical trout-lilies, gaywings,
bluets, wild oats, goldthread,
even more golden cowslips,
these and all their cousins
received and released,
fraying into the greater greening.
Gone.

April

Spring can happen any time now,
minting life faster than we can spend it,
turning any day's corner into the new.
With thaw and eaves' drip
seeps a fleeting almost purple haze
across the all-around-us hills,
told bolder by willows already yellow
as marmalade, as honey, as the sun
warming tentative hobo birds
and hatless, coatless, bootless us.

Cardinal: A Field Guide

There—your—how-can-you-be-so-red streak
comes to rest against the soggy snow all around.
Surprising, your showing up at all in this not-quite-Spring,
so sharp in foggy air, on sopping ground,
repeating the meant-to-be-paired-that-may-not-be
bleak—note—heard in minor songless sound.
Both the bird and the lip-lisping boy with the book
listening for the ought-to-be-answer nowhere found.

Your quick static-not-static tilt,
while your flat black eye goes everywhere;
your whispered twist of *tcship, tcship,*
beak stabbing at the tangled alder;
your slurred whistle that will not come to rest,
tcship, she was supposed to meet me here.

Winter Afternoon

Sometimes, like just now,
putting damp clothes
in this prosaic dryer,
the inside of me
is whirling around
in togetherness with you.

Walks.
Winter light.
The pond.
a world of black and white
spinning in my inner air.

Please ask, and I will offer loudly,
because gladly, this,
picked lovingly like lint
from an old but favorite sweater:
something new and more than words,
this having back one winter afternoon.

Mourning Doves

They don't desert us in the winter.
They share pointless things with us,
constantly clearing their throats,
morning and evening,
measuring questions.

Snowshoeing

You are in the wind today
pouring the cold down the mountain,
shaping the snow.

You are in the snow
drifting along the road,
sifting the field,
sculpting each breaker,
separately,
to a static brink.

You go wherever the wind goes
for a long long moment,
then suddenly you are back,
speaking the very kisses
my snowshoes print.

Now you wander ahead again
into the white.
The snow beneath me
and the sky above me
are one,
entirely light.

Skating at 60

It's good to know
you can get some things back.
My old skates hanging
in the dimness of the woodshed—
they'd become invisible really,
their once oiled uppers supple no longer,
gone starchy and feltlike,
the blades running to rust
like the nail they were hanging from—
my old skates cleaned up nicely.

Skating again.
Hurling myself around the pond.
I'd forgotten to remember
the wild swing and lean of it,
now writing wide full uncials all over the ice,
entering again the wingèd time
and finding such majuscule grace still in me.

II

Nobody Told Me

Be Careful At Antietam

These sepia spirits of boys who look about fifteen
in poses strict as the parts in their hair
make me wonder what they had for breakfast,
wish to see their smiles over milk and molasses after supper.

Monuments.
I'm back at the Visitor Center
after trudging the fields all around
in a hat-wrenching April wind,
reading a brochure about a battlefield reenactment.

Go ahead. Accuse me
of having too much imagination.
Nobody told me. I wasn't warned.
I didn't know a certain hardness was needed

to think about the state of the hay then,
the noise, the smell, the thirst,
the blood browning all over these same boys
we see in the arranged pictures here,
lying ruined in the trodden asters and corn
with their older, wiser handlers.
I won't be back.

Little Things

She knows why
she's forever sending someone home
with slips of this and that
from some grandmother's potted plant,
sending them off to live in the worlds
of other people's windows.
She knows why.

❧

Out back, her old man
rolls an exactly squared
top and bottom
round and heavy
block of oak
out of his woodpile.
Take her home with you, he says.
She's a beauty.

❧

Much of a lifetime,
uncountable cords of stovewood
and miles of kindling sticks
have crossed her since.
Bonus piles of sweet starter chips
like flaky talus mound her sides.
Rough, axe scarred, forever.
Thanks, old man,
she's a beauty.

Prodigal Father Celebrates Son's Homecoming

So the boy'd made some mistakes.
Wasted some bucks.
Gone up in smoke.
He knew enough to drag his ass back home, didn't he?
Made his solid-as-Gibraltar brother green.
He'd hoped his old man would have him back—
but giving him a big party,
that taught him something.
Things weren't so bad after all.

He wondered if the old man'd heard
the story about the sad son-of-a-bitch
he'd bailed out that time.
Bad news.
He'd felt the sting of it.
He'd rather not have been noticed,
used to seeing their noses out of joint
whenever he was in the neighborhood.
He despised them right back
for their weak sneers,
the greasy cowards,
pretending they didn't even see
the poor bastard in the ditch,
pissy, beat up, sleeping it off.
But he'd braved it.
As if it were charity!
Just saw it as something he could do.
After all, only his hands got dirty.
He didn't think his old man knew about it, though.
Old news.

Sometimes I get everything all mixed up.
Parables now on sale. Two for the price of one.
Good news. Like father, like son.

Standing By Anna,
her friend dead in Iraq

I came right away.
We walked out here,
the ground frozen,
slicked with wet leaves
along the low stream.

How your closed mouth worked.

Cold rain
made the planks
of the bridge glisten.
Water drops
along the railing
hung separately
in the path light.
Now and again
a drop strung a trickle down,
a little liquid spilling.

Hiking Out To Brave Boat Harbor

We accumulate them as we go.
All we can hold.
These:
crossing the island,
a mile through the woods,
through the light and the dark,
bare to the knees.
You lag behind a little. Stop.
I catch on. Turn back.
Hand raised, you listen,
shin deep in the fern.

Eyes big, I'm witness
to your sussing out the song birds,
the deep-woods birds,
the sometimes heard but never seen birds.
Some simple sustained sibilance
spilling from your lips
and they come,
all the near twigs soon occupied,
then your arms, your shoulders.
Better than walking on the water
we're on our way to see,
your transfiguration into some
St. Francis-of-the-Denim-Cutoffs
come to life on the old woods trail.

Friend making special memories
from a summer you were just passing through,
taking a break on our hike across the island,
you're gone where so many of the boys went
in the not-so-gay eighties.
These are more than I can hold.
Like you shedding the birds and moving on,
I shed this much for those
who listen all the way to the end.

Dressing Gaia

The bulldozers nudge their way around the old sow,
rooting in the landfill.
They are sculpting the rubbish.
Just one of the countless ways
they are getting her ready for the big day.

Untroubled, all allowing in their wallow,
she suffocates in the offal of her greedy children.
They are packing it in.

Will confetti fly among the stars
in a kind of nuptial surprise
when this ball is ripped apart?
Things may come around right next time,
she wheezes, as she tells us,
there is time enough
for other marriages, and births, too,
when new suns start.

The Pause

We rest, lungs heaving,
loud in the silence of the undercut.
We stand or lean on torn slabs,
frost peeled and slipped from the ledge's face,
on end, as they happen, some stacked but broken plates.

Standing among them in the closeness,
grown still with the water seeping
over the dolmen's moist chin,
we are sinking into the source of the silence,
the mute mass wearing in weather and weight.

Places where the skin of the stone is torn
show us the earth's bones and blood:
riotous quartz running in granite,
veins spitting up crystals,
seams cleaving the rock,
splitting sight up to the eyes staring inward—
as outwardly,
the mind metamorphosed sees itself,
erupts at the surface, frozen, in solid surprise.

Watercolor

This is no violet to blue scheme,
quaint décor of jonquil
or tired fuchsia,
with once in a while
an exciting sexual red,
arranged, as the master says,
by a perhaps hand.

No. These are the colors.
We can't tell the moment's
exactly coming
with wide awesome hues
into the new spectrum,
but here they are, flowing
like the desert's quick Spring,
swelling the cells of light,
flooding the surface,
floating in the pulse of the prism.

Getting It

Safe now from the glut of prosetry
you remember fading light, stumbling
over the reeking (is this a?) landscape?
shuddering in your rags,
telling of snares escaped,
teetering from hummock to hummock,
trudging free of the swamp at last.

Safe now and curled in comfort,
listening to the sap-laden logs
wailing in the fire, you ask
where did all that sad—was it? music? go?

The day will come
like the furling unfurling sea
nuzzling the brave boats at noon—
where have they all gone and come back to?—

The day will come
when you knuckle your eyes clear,
glimpse the saving once-in-a-while,
the loss that makes you more;
see the birds dipping in the green gloom,
hear what goes on idling in the blood,
heart left ajar.

In The Poem For The Muse

Eructavit cor meum verbum bonum. Ps. 44

In Wonderman Will's sonnets are
bare ruined choirs where late the sweet birds sang.
In cummings there are things
which I cannot touch because they are too near.
So pay attention.
This is not about
exciting boyfriends and exotic vacations.
This is about the famous fire in the mind.
Not the stuff *museums* are made of.

You will not find them *there,*
these women
who come to us like goddesses
from their long-since ruined temples of glory—
not like echoes hovering at the edges
of tattered old schoolbooks.
Maybe you want to look them up.
You *can* revive them.
Have any one of them walk right up to you
and tell you how Erato must feel about her
millennia-long confusion with you-know-who;
or Calliope The Brave, trapped and trivialized
through centuries of endless circus stints.
Now, you know, they are somewhere *musing*
about where to place the next *Apostrophe—*
in the margin, perhaps, with you.

O Aoede, first of The Failing Sisters,
we so crave and dread the fire.
You do not make us join you in your making.
Of all your heart-stretching gifts
the greatest is this reaching out your hand to us
in the burning silence.
When I take it
you pull me into such heat,
inspiring under ribs expanding for breath
my heart erupts with the right word.

Reading Cavafy

You'd give anything for it.
You show me how.
We are brushing against dim walls,
going alone together
into those shadowy places
no one ever visits.
Ask anyone.

Hidden behind the frame's edge,
how we long for it,
leaning out, just to see,
just this once more,
how it used to be:
peering *into* pictures
of gone-by beauty,
of urgent youth
thinning into the gloom.
Ahhh!

Wanting Comfort

After your long morning of moving through cold rooms
I'd place you here,
somewhere on the far side of noon,
lying in a dip, out of the wind,
in weak sun, and the almost-warm,
crumpled, copper-falling-into-flakes of last year's ferns.
We two spooned, you lurching in my arms, looking up
at daytime's awkward surprise,
the battered face of the moon.
In a dip. Out of the wind. Me wanting you safe
from every *Oh no. Not now. Not so soon.*

       Wailing from your very middle
       words wrung out first and last.
       Come back. Come back.
       Your shaking shoulders never done.

Hearts of Gold

A sculptor might have caught them
in the very clay they were made of.
George and Alice.
So we would see.
This is how they are still available.
His name *was* George,
but everyone knew him as Unc.
There was just the one dragon in his life
and he never did slay it.
One was too many and a hundred weren't enough.
He was a saint anyway. You'll see.

Well into my hoping-not-to-be-noticed-
I'll-just-shuffle-right-by,
I'd see him through the beer joint window
on one of the several stools
I know he considered his very own.
I see it all in amber:
the always many random bottles
and many half-filled glasses,
the thick light through the window
and the cycling neon script—
I'd swear it was all in amber
though I know it really couldn't have been.

Then Alice,
always referred to as his floosie
(but never in her presence; and yes,
the term really was current back then)
always referred to as his floosie
by the same everyone-else-around-me
who treated her with great, and I think
sincere but-to-me-puzzling kindness
whenever Unc brought her around,
which was surprisingly often.
A bonding born in beer joint heaven,
they had their own curious kind of
taking care of each other.
Hearts of gold. Yes, I said *hearts.*
But Alice was pretty far gone.
She didn't last. They didn't.

Well, he had to land somewhere.
In the end one of his sisters took him in.
Sat him in the front room,
on the table at his wrist
his now one-at-a-time stubbies
(they really were called stubbies in those days,
those squat little ten ouncers)
his one at a time stubbies: beer bottle amber again.
I'm glad now we hardly ever glimpsed
the not-so-pretty behind the scenes.
She was good at that. Matante.

The wisdom had always been
that he just couldn't help himself.
And by now he really couldn't.
Are you ready for this?
I'm not. Not really.
With a little reminding whenever I popped in—
not many bothered popping in any more—
with a little reminding
he'd place me exactly. For a while.
Then we'd begin all over again.

I'm reduced to a grateful heart,
(I can say *heart* if I want to)
a grateful heart
for all the fun that flowed from Unc
while we were growing up.
This keeps coming back to me:
playing ball, getting a hit,
he'd always throw the bat off into the blue—
he just couldn't help himself—
he'd throw the bat off into the blue,
then he'd run like hell!

Now you see *why:*
why I remember this for him
and wonder what he forgot instead.

Balancing Act,
for T.H. White

I remember my first time perfectly.
Everyone does.
This book that launched a thousand reads
was dinner and supper and dessert to me.
How weak I would be without it.
For growing up in Camelot, a Future King,
for getting me over games mania
into the real magic of the immediate world,
thank you.

Books. They come and go by the armsful
except this one shelf's worth,
this special one among them
I've been learning by heart most of my life.
It's never the same twice, or again,
like all the other improbable things
that fill my shelves
with Knowledge of the World,
giving this strange poise, beyond balance.
Like a seventh sense.
Thank you.

At The Barn Window

her frantic feathers whitter
and scratch at the glass,
behind bars,
impossibly suspended flutter

but can-do moving smoothly in me,
slowly stepping near,
raising the lower sash
smoothly, arms up

so she just dipping down
and diving out
into the desperately longed for,
smoothly, wings up

Remains Of An Ancient Oak

The soil is alive and seething,
stringing cells together in teeming ceaselessness,
as the smooth waking nut shoulders crumbs,
heaves itself up in urgent crinkled veining,
from earth and air becoming the tree flowing singly,
from darkest drinking root
to farthest dripping twig—
each tip's end telling the truth—
from each reaching vessel winding back,
building the oak's great heart,
the living layer beneath the bark,

to raging arms ripped in centuries of wind
shedding its great limbs in ruinous age,
making new and godly ground below,
a richer, sweeter bed
for the embryo we worship,
the seed, the symbol, the source.

Sunset In The Woods

There is no sky
in this late-in-the-day light,
saffron glowing
across the gently folded
mossy hollows
sloping to the guessed-at spring below.
There is no sky caught
near the sinking green bed,
thinning light
picking over the twiggy litter,
counting the amber needles and cones,
the last far reach of it
held a minute,
thickening into shadow,
tucked away and let go.

III

No Absence Can Be Real

The Blue Chair

I come home from work
and find you on the porch,
papers spread,
painting its fine
up and down spindles.

You run the brush
along the rungs in long slow strokes,
on your knees,
the chair balancing you tipping the chair,
deep in your important play.

Now you are far away.
The blue chair is anywhere around the house
saying over and over
no absence can be real
when I am caught in this bright minute.

Mighty you kneeling over me.
Me gripped in that same strong and easy way.
This will always be your chair.

While Weeding

The garden misses you.
Not the flowers.
Everyone thinks it's about the flowers.
Well it's not.
Oh,
they're still there, flashing
and dripping their countless colors
all day long,
and standing precisely
in the negative under the moon at night.
No.
It's about this inner place
that melts and fuses longing
into somewhere else we go.
You know where I'll be.
The place where even the birds
are used to me missing you.
Their just perceptible chatter
is all about wondering where you are.

Constellation

Under the circling night sky
always your body against me singing
you are the one I come to life for
dizzy under the stars.

Imagine my blood running everywhere in me
reading your skin with hands hot with it,
or only your fingers to my lips
the universe explodes
and we're spinning in the dance.

Reflections

I am dripping and dissolving with the moon
in the luminous haze over the water.

I am trying to find my voice.
I want to talk to you.
I want to tell you we can swim to the moon.
We can let love go in the deepest stars of the night sky,
scattering light in the lonely cold—so hot! so close!

But there is only the broken face of the pool
in its frame of granite bones.

The wind is raking the water around me.
The shattering mirror slanting away
keeps spilling at the pool's edge.
I want to hold you just a moment,
trying to catch what it mutters at its stone lip.

What Can Never Be

Locked and laboring beyond pleasing
in our terrible wondrous heat,
or lying stripped and spent—
in my mad and holy place within
you cannot see—I know
you take them all to bed with you, with me.
Already lonely, your discarded heart
mirrors my own matching caution
of their careless inner bashing of you.

Still, I will cradle tenderly your hurt,
and feed your phoenix hunger for a while.
But I can only tell your bare and painful beauty
what can never be:
though the strength of arms in utmost wanting
ties us fast together,
I cannot hold your heart invulnerable,
or keep you safe inside my fragile self.

Sea Point Beach

My tongue was dumb
as my clumsy feet
when you gave the sea suds
your hand, a pebble your ocean.

I only stuttered
when the sun broke out,
but pleased you to sing a wind
that swept away each note.

You had every right
to run that soft stretch of sand,
broad-surging brine
sudden-lapping your shoe.

You had every right to break on me—
running at your side,
in that same daylight only an elbow away—
your whole ocean, your whole tide, intensely.

Harpist

Take the still harp of my heart
in hands again moving with music
'til now unheard.
Harp a night of notes,
grace notes,
dripping and pooling,
moving with music,
mingling
silent stars and singing strings.

Like the ripple of the brook
cupping and pouring
over the swirling starfull mirror,
see stars trickle
through uncurling
carefully opening fingers,
spilling pebbly points of light,
mingling
warm blackness and shimmering sight.
And streaming through the swelling circle
of the flowing firmament
now rushing and rising
in hands again moving,
leap and drop
in a fall of notes,
grace notes,
gathering and pooling
in the luster of the riddle.

O day of delight
in the darkness of night
binding in tremulous time
all blindness and sight,
when you please to,
as only you can press,
lay gently your fingers,
the flat of your hand upon,
still again these strings,
make me mute.

Found Innocent

So tough when you need to be, little brother,
gone away city boy,
gone far from the home place
at the end of the road,
but back now briefly. Rare visit.

Talking up to me in your old way,
your just-hanging-around way—
me puzzled, protective.
You haven't broken anything this time.

No. You've come back to tell an old woe,
dredging up something,
somehow, both damp and dry,
something from your boyhood days
playing in the old root cellar.
Something about the caught
and for curiosity kept salamander
placed at the bottom of an old potato box—
but for weeks forgot, then after found
in gray and dusty grief and guilt.
I see it all in your eyes slammed shut.

Such miles of dread, staying all this time
alone at the end of your own road.
Years of particular kindness
a sort of painstaking penance.
So now you're back at the home place,
taking the rap, emptying out the bins,
sweeping the old cellar clean.

Stay another day or two
before going back to that
blotting-it-all-out noise.
You must see my eyes glad-stricken
at this knowing, little brother,
this knowing why you can do no wrong.

Lil

What would you say,
you of the too much wine too often?
Aunt to the neighborhood.
Off to the mill each morning.
Hugger. Glad Maker.
No fun to be had without.
You of the careful blanket
over my ear each night.

Well do I know
there are no words.
But I can hear you, amazed:
Well, come on, huh?
You're not writing a poem for me!

Mowing

The edge of your eyebrow curving
whets me,
as myself standing on an edge,
standing on the cut
with the uncut grass before me,
I draw this stone sure
along this scythe's edge glinting,
then set the blade
to snatching at the bloom again.

Dreading Spring

We're walking up to the old bridge.
You've been wanting to.

See how everything is changed:
the winter's rust in the blackberry canes,
no summer, no purple left in them;
the rain-beaten road gravel
scraped and ribbed
like a crumpled map—
unreadable, rearranged.

It all happens so fast,
as if the road were pouring away behind us
like the cursive ribbon of the brook
we glimpse through the trees
rushing down to the crossing we're coming to.

This merest grass at the road's edge,
this Spring we're almost in,
will have its own green,
as winter had its safe and only white.
You're already pointing out the sheen
of even greener shoots ahead
at the farthest edge of the guardrail,
the vanishing point in our line of sight.

I'll stay on the bridge
counting the moss cushions on the boulders below,
how many, how few,
watching the water pouring away before me,
while you cross over and continue
beyond the bridge and out of view.

Standing beside this crusty bank of old snow
can I be wanting winter back?
That would be new.
Let me just say,
See you later. Be safe.
And so you go.

Spring Peepers

I will kill this death with Spring
and let it go on straining waves of sound
to the other ear.

I will be fierce in this,
leaving the useless words for love
that never was—
each word a leaf, each leaf a green lie—
leaving them all finally corroding
in the slow but solvent sun.

Tomorrow is the most I have ever dared
in this new glad land,
entering the night swamp,
learning from hearing only
what will come, and from what oozings,
in the ear-splitting dark.

I am already risen in their million voices pulsing,
in their ragged, waking, screaming
this shrill joy ! shrill joy!

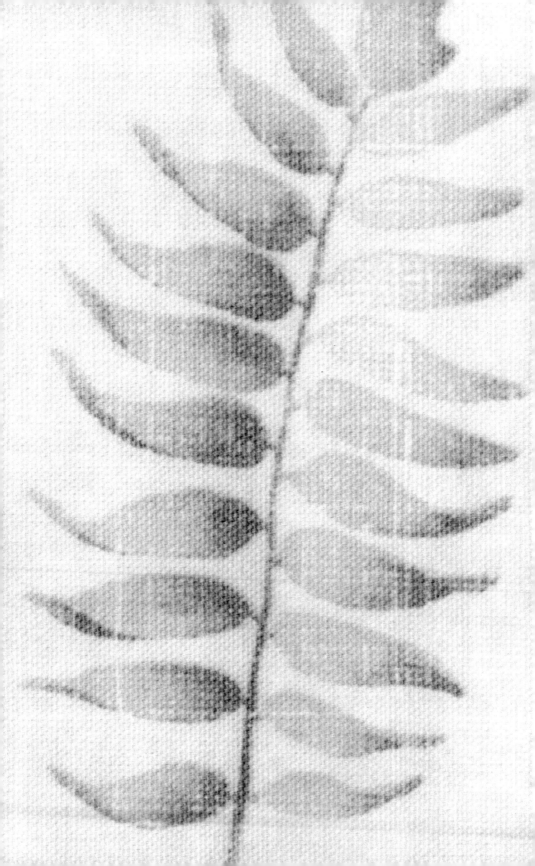

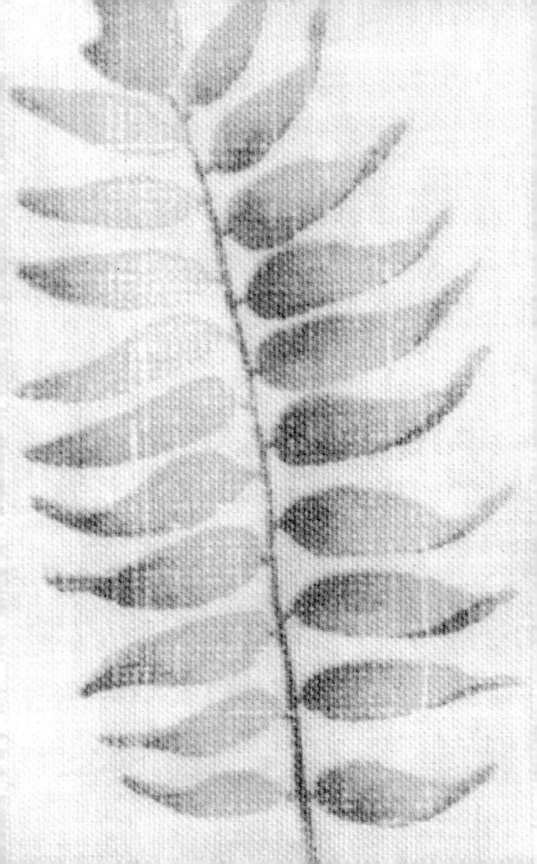

IV

So All At Sea

Lost At Sea

So. You've gone after him at last.
So much for giving up.
So much for letting go.
All that never knowing,
and now you finally do.

As fast into your late sleep
as he so early tucked to his
for a twenty-something sailor, child—
you, too, so all at sea,
and all those years apart.
You always said that he could not be never found.

Where did your pain go
when you were done with it?
Tossed and drowned like his
in the endless rocking surge,
or floated slowly out
on a calm and boundless swell?

Ah, no. Never mind.
Lifting your lost boy up at last
from that soft sea bed but never cold
you insisted must be his—
slipping away anywhere now,
or nowhere, together, catching the tide.

Meeting

Nobody comes here anymore.
Now everyone's business
is over at the new Municipal Complex
where my poems and *dreams* can't go.
At least I don't think they can.
Maybe that's why I'm here
seeing everything sideways.
What an odd place to meet.
Or maybe not.
Nobody comes here anymore.

The Old Town Hall's doorstones
tip this way and that,
not much used anymore.
I can't believe my luck.
I've been looking for you
everywhere but here
in the not-quite-right.
Somehow you've made it
up to the—is it?—third step, it seems.
Or maybe you're near me at the bottom.
Impossible to tell
in this slanted world of reckless joy.

How can I know you're about to take
the words right out of my mouth?
Displaced,
you turn to me,
you say,
Is it really you?

Bertha

Memory gropes, chooses,
picks a morning 'cause it's handy
and you are in it.
Pumpkins on doorsteps
orange and vineless,
a hayrake rusting down
in the corner of a sloping field,
other ledge outcroppings
under woodbine red, or sumac.
This land October unblesses.
Like the turning of a shoulder to me
this time defriends.
What I see now,
this day of damped fires,
all the long long thought of it,
is but the waiting.

I hardly know you,
dozing in the kitchen rocker,
lap spread with busy trifles
saved against this spell.
Then sudden-waking,
quickly wrinkling lip to lash,
reaching up and reaching back,
pinning up your scolding locks,
still getting ready.

The work of eighty years
's a game of tic-tac-toe
scoring spots and creases.
In the threading of a needle
I see your hands.

Ice Out

Just between the two of us
always the last week of April
the ice goes off the lake—
always the last week of April.

Have I really been all these years
coming up here again
for the long view of the lake?
The rows of stones have broadened,
but I have no trouble finding your place.
Here is Your One Name among the many.
Marked just below the others, just for you:
their dau. Then the dates.

Just between the two of us,
we're old enough to know better.
And we do. We know
memory is not what the heart wants.
It wants to be with the ice,
slowly warming in the cold water.
It wants to go.

Dialog

1

This morning the river is a slack ribbon.
The wide silt slick wetly mirrors
the ridge and rolling fields on the other side.
I think you must be over there somewhere,
out of sight around the bend,
beyond the green and silver tidewater winding.
I want to tell you this grove of pine and oak
I'm grooming was someone's pasture once,
later left to brambles and brush,
now grown to a stand of final harder woods.
All the farm this side of the river
is newly planted with decently distanced houses,
the grove a neighborly screen.
I can think you shrug and spread your hands: so?
But I can't be glad of this work for folks
who count on making their own little wilderness.
Not for any amount and so much an hour.

2

Unquiet, reluctant,
I go on raking away the thatch of needles,
stripping away the thickly layered leaves,
lower pages gone all porous,
almost done their dissolving.
I am everywhere exposing
the bones of old junipers,
knotted joints and bony elbows—
in this synaptic instant I see them as they were,
the lazy junipers leaning outward
in shallow bowls of blue-green prickle
reflecting the river in blue and silver bristle
in the wide light before the trees came—
now bony elbows pinned and buried in the litter,
bared and brought to the light again:
kaleidoscope of fleshless arms
spindling in the shade,
feathering into vanished whorls.

69

3

In that last snap I have of you,
accident of you taken by surprise,
hobbling out to the field with an old hoe,
you nearly ninety and with so much to do,
keeping the place from growing up—
sharing visions of your grandmothers
grubbing with mattocks, planting around the stumps
in this same long-since smoothed field—
you say you mustn't get caught going backward.
So you pry them up and rip them out
by their roots, the first invaders here,
sappy poplars, green and fast.
While you're at it you pause, lament
how they won't be here in the Spring,
fringing out so soft, with their own green,
your sign always that Spring is really here this time.
I never see their beauty but through you,
the poplars fringing out.
By splicing in this telling point
our dialog begins again.

4

The slow years slip down the river on the misty tide.
You've been gone a long time.
And yet it seems you're always dropping in,
catching me at some unholy work.
I see you shrug and spread your hands again: so?
This is you in inner whisper given back,
speaking for the junipers as one returning
from that dim exile over there:
they should be beautiful and hidden,
slowly burning beneath the leaves
beside the blue and silver water.

5

The ribbon of the river
threads away in the long twilight.
The tide has come and gone again.
The junipers are piled
and burning on the riverbank.
I can hear your closest voice,
see your spread and empty hands.
The fire sags and shifts,
topples in a wild flurry.
I have to let you go again
in the shimmering heat and smoke.
Something in me rushes up
in the great fiery draft,
greets the first furious trembling stars.
Like your smarting eyes, my eyes
smearing brilliants white-hot and red,
blurring sparks snapping to cinders,
ashes drifting across the darkening aerial Styx.

Snickerdoodles

You've had some fun in ninety years.
Picked lots of daisies, you say.
But curling down now and reaching
to the bottom of you—you just can't.
And so you lure me over
with coffee and cookies,
the boy next door, forty-plus me.

I cradle your feet between my thighs,
one at a time,
clip and file,
one at a time, the ends
of these private, tight little toes.
You're knitting away the whole time.
I wonder if you hear the snicking
of the needles or the ticking of the old clock
on the shelf behind you.

Mulling over these humble runes
I see the generations rolling
anonymously through the millennia,
gentled by such frailty and care as this.
Soon I leave you under your lamp,
your book on your knees,
your hand raised in thanks and good-night.

Home. Later.
Getting the pillow just right,
slipping into sleep,
I see the withered edge of the moon
through the open summer window,
and another window opens behind my eyes:
I see you in your chair,
your book on your knees,
hand raised,
pausing to turn the last page,
reaching for quiet.